Note Designer:

A Simple Step-by-Step Guide to

Writing Your Psychotherapy Progress Notes

Time-saving, ready-to-use outlines, examples, and phrases included

Patricia C. Baldwin, Ph.D.
Clinical Psychologist
www.notedesigner.com

Table of Contents

To my family, for their support and good humour:
Mark, Larry, and little Maxwell.

Introduction

When I was starting out as a psychologist in private practice I agonized over the issue of keeping psychotherapy progress notes. Though we were given some general direction during my training, I remained overwhelmed whenever I was staring down at the blank page after a session with a client. Typically, I would end up writing far too much as I tried to capture the complexity of what had gone on between my client and myself and the many themes and processes at play. Frustrated, I would then sometimes neglect my notes for a time and end up feeling anxious and guilty regarding my work and professionalism. As my practice grew and I began seeing many more clients, the situation only became more unmanageable.

In speaking with a number of colleagues, I was pleased to find that I was not the only one experiencing this and discovered that many of my fellow clinicians also felt confused and conflicted about how to maintain their psychotherapy records. Indeed, one of my colleagues disclosed having almost given up on record keeping altogether! To add to the anxiety was the apprehension about being inspected by my professional order and to be found lacking. After some time struggling with this issue, I began exploring various recommendations about how to write appropriate session notes. These guidelines are a result of my explorations whereby I attempt to distil the most essential features and summarize the most important elements of appropriate record keeping in a user-friendly and effective manner.

Just to clarify, when I mention "psychotherapy session notes" or "psychotherapy progress notes" I do not mean the detailed process notes that one writes to explore a session in depth – such as what one brings to a supervisor or for one's study of the psychotherapy process. That type of note, though essential to our work, is far too revealing and detailed, and often includes our more personal reflections and conjecture regarding a case

– this is not the type of information to be kept in the client's official file. An important reason that these process notes are excluded from the official record is that they may reveal information that, when taken out of context or without the requisite professional understanding, may be hurtful or even damaging to the wellbeing of the client such as when read by the client himself or herself or by a third party who may gain access to the clinical record. Indeed, most regulatory bodies (such as those in the United States that are regulated by the Health Insurance Portability and Accountability Act - HIPAA) do advise that this type of information be explicitly left out of your official clinical files. Whether we agree with it or not, a client's official file can, under certain circumstances (i.e., court ordered subpoena), be accessed by third parties. Because of this, the full confidentiality of our clinical records is not something we can entirely protect (even though one might argue that we should; Levin, Furlong, & O'Neil, 2003). As a result, we are faced with the difficult task of needing to document our clinical work and yet to try and do so in a manner that will be as protective of the patient's privacy and confidentiality as is possible. The integrity of our work and our capacity to foster a therapeutic space within which individuals can freely explore their anxieties, pains, experiences and behavioral difficulties of course rests upon it being conducted in a confidential and private setting.

So then, what do we put in a client's official file and how can we discipline ourselves to write and maintain appropriate psychotherapy session notes? In the pages that follow, I am going to explain and demonstrate (using examples, templates, and sample statements) what I have discovered to be a helpful, efficient and structured way to write psychotherapy progress notes. The ideas I present are derived from several sources including my exploration of the literature on record keeping and note writing, consultation with colleagues and professional orders, as well as from my own 20 years of record keeping experience. The book should be useful to mental health professionals in private practice, clinics, and other service centers. Students, interns and junior colleagues in particular will benefit from getting an early start on good psychotherapy record keeping and in establishing and maintaining their files without undue stress and anxiety.

Before proceeding to our discussion of Intake Reports, Progress Notes and Termination Summaries, it is important to reinforce that once you have successfully completed these documents they have to be stored in a secure location. It is, of course, part of our professional and ethical responsibility to ensure and protect the privacy and confidentiality of all information regarding our clients and their treatment. Though this might seem like one of the simpler aspects of our work, in this age of laptop computers, tablets, cell phones, text messages, e-mails and the internet it is worth some careful consideration. The traditional method of securely storing clinical records involves placing all printed documentation in a locked filing cabinet in a secure location. Before the use of personal computers this was the only option available and for those clinicians who prefer handwriting their notes this is generally the recommended approach. In my opinion this method remains the most straightforward for securing the protection of patient information. Though I do know of some colleagues who continue to write their notes out longhand, more and more clinicians are using electronic devices with which to compose and store their documents. Whenever a clinician uses an electronic device for the writing and storage (temporary or otherwise) of clinical material they must ensure that their electronic device is at minimum protected by a secure password such that only the clinician can gain access to the clinical files, and ideally the files themselves are effectively encrypted. As with other recommendations suggested in these guidelines, please be sure to inform yourself and follow the specific regulations regarding record storage as stipulated by your professional order and/or in your clinical setting and jurisdiction.

Finally, though this book is designed to stand alone as a helpful resource for initiating and maintaining your record keeping, I will also mention here that my computer-programmer colleague and I developed a psychotherapy note writing software program (Note Designer) to help make the task a little quicker and easier. The sample statements that you will find at the end of the book and many of the templates and sample progress notes included in the chapters are excerpted from our software program. Blank templates and other materials are available for free on our website at http://www.notedesigner. com/book/ .

Note: Recommendations and examples presented are intended to provide a general overview of how to write psychotherapy progress notes and do not constitute nor can they substitute for legal counsel or official guidelines mandated by any particular professional order or other regulatory body; please be sure to consult and familiarize yourself with the guidelines and rules regarding record keeping in your particular mental health field and/or as stipulated by your professional order.

Chapter 1

Opening a File: The Intake Report

The first type of documentation that is needed in any psychotherapy file is the Intake Report. This is a general overview of the information collected during the assessment period of the prospective psychotherapy treatment. The Intake Report documents certain essential pieces of information as is required by most institutions and professional orders or colleges. Below is an example of the types of identifying information that normally begins a clinical file and the Intake Report. Following that you will find an outline of the main sections of the report with a brief description of what each section should contain. A sample of a completed Intake Report, very loosely based on a file from my clinical practice, is included at the end of the chapter along with a ready-to-use template. A free, downloadable Intake Report template is also available on our website at http://www.notedesigner.com/book/ .

INTAKE REPORT

Name: **Date of Report:**
Date of Birth: **Address:**
Telephone numbers: **Okay to leave message?:**
Emergency Contact Information: **Marital Status:**
Occupation: **Living Arrangement:**
Referral Source:
Date of Intake Session(s):

Brief Description of the Patient:

This section often begins with some introductory comments and/or behavioral observations regarding the client's (or "patient's", as you prefer) appearance, initial presentation, and manner of interacting with the therapist and the therapeutic environment. For instance, you may state that "the client appeared anxious, spoke quickly, and avoided eye contact with the therapist". Be careful to refrain from comments that could come across as personal opinion or as evaluative in tone (e.g., "the client didn't bother to remove his boots upon entering the office, even after I asked him" versus "the client kept his boots on during the interview, despite being requested to remove them"). The idea here is to keep the tone observational and dispassionate. Always keep in mind that your client may read his or her file and it is important that there is nothing in the file that could be harmful or hurtful for the client to read. Keeping the report observational in style also limits and keeps in check the inclusion of our own potential underlying personal biases and preferences.

Presenting Difficulties:

The main content then moves to a description of what brings the client to be seeking help at this time. Typically, this will involve restating what the client reports to you as his or her reason for wanting help. It is important that this portrays an account of the client's perspective.

It is sometimes helpful to use actual quotes from what the client stated and to use phrases such as "The client reported…", "According to the client…" or "The client stated that…." The point here to remember is not to include *your interpretation* of what the client is saying but mostly *your observation* of what the client is telling you. This is especially important when the client is also referring to the actions and characteristics of other people (e.g., "The client's mother has numerous extramarital affairs and cheats on her taxes" versus "The client stated that she believes her mother has numerous extramarital affairs and cheats on her taxes"). Bear in mind that unless you've actually seen and assessed the client's family members/colleagues/friends you are only able to recount the perspective of the client.

Reminder: As in all sections of the report and the client's file, be careful not to include any proper names of people the client mentions (the use of an initial is a better option).

History of the Presenting Difficulties:

In this section, you briefly recount the history of the client's presenting problems. For instance, this might include events leading up to the beginning of the difficulties, some background regarding the environmental or social conditions faced by the client that may be relevant to the presenting difficulties, details regarding the first appearance of the difficulties, and any past attempts at seeking help and their outcome(s).

As described in the section above, when reporting on what the client has told you, try to maintain an observational or journalistic style. If you want to include any statements regarding your own understanding or broader interpretation of what the client is reporting, it is important to preface these with phrases such as "It appears as though…", "There was some suggestion that…", "I had the impression that the client was struggling to describe…", "Though the client reported having fully recovered after her first depressive crisis, her difficulty maintaining her relationships and hobbies suggests that the depression may have persisted". While on the topic of how to include your own clinical impressions and interpretations, I suggest that you try as best you can to support all of your own impressions by including the information you are using to get there. By doing this, you are strengthening the validity of your report and will help others (including the client) better understand your conclusions if there arises the need to share the report.

Significant Life History and Background Information:

Here you summarize the background information and life history of the client as based on your intake interview(s). For instance, you here include details regarding the client's family of origin, siblings, significant interpersonal and romantic relationships and children. As well, you might include here a summary of how the client described his or her family members, childhood experiences, and past traumas or difficult experiences. You might also here include a description of the client's educational and work history as well as a description of any hobbies, interests or other information important to understanding the client as derived from your interview.

It is usually helpful to organize this section into paragraphs that fit the different aspects of the client's history. You might even use subheadings to lend further structure (e.g., Family Background, Educational and Work History, Childhood and Adolescence, Developmental History, Marital and Family Relations, Sexuality, Hobbies and Interests, etc.).

As described above, be sure to be mindful to keep the tone journalistic, nonjudgmental and non-evaluative. Again, make good use of phrases such as "The client reported that...", "According to the client…", "The client further explained…." And again, if you feel it is important to include your own impressions, use a style that signals that this is your conjecture: "In speaking so briefly and positively about his family, I had the impression that he may have been uncomfortable disclosing more personal information at this time", etc.

Significant Medical History:

In this section, you briefly describe the significant medical/physical issues reported by the client during the intake assessment (as a reminder: it is generally recommended that a mental health practitioner take a medical history as part of the intake assessment). Unless you are also a medical practitioner (and so may have reason to do otherwise), here you are basically recording what the client has reported. For example, we will record things such as reported past illnesses, surgeries, hospitalizations, chronic health conditions, accidents that required medical attention as well as the client's overall tendency towards ill physical health and somatic symptoms (e.g., frequent headaches, nausea, constipation, etc.). Medications that the client is taking are also noted in this section; whether you need include the dosages and exact names of the client's medications will depend on the nature of the case, the requirements of the institution or jurisdiction where you are working, and your own professional credentials.

Clinical Observations and Impressions:

This section is a place for the clinician to record (in greater detail than what was stated under "presenting difficulties") his or her observations and impressions of how the client behaves, comes across, interacts, and responds to the clinical situation. This might also include the overall results of any testing that was conducted during the intake processes (e.g., Beck Depression Inventory, Symptom Checklist, Mini-Mental exam, etc.). As well, you would include here the nature and results of your risk assessment (if deemed necessary). The information provided in this section will serve as the basis for your Diagnostic Impressions and Preliminary Clinical Formulation that will follow. As in other sections of the report, please be careful not to inadvertently use a pejorative tone or state anything that might be hurtful or harmful if the client were to read the report.

Diagnostic Impressions:

As based on your clinical observations and impressions, here you briefly state your diagnostic impressions. If you are a psychiatrist or medical professional or are in a state or province where you have the mandate to use DSM/ICD diagnoses this is where you record your preliminary diagnosis/diagnoses and corresponding DSM/ICD code(s) (if necessary or required). It is important to substantiate your diagnosis or diagnostic impression with the data you observed (as outlined in other sections of the report). It is often helpful to use phrases such as "The client's clinical presentation is consistent with a diagnosis of ..." or "The client meets the DSM criteria for a diagnosis of ..." as a means of conveying your impression. For those clinicians who do not use official diagnostic categories, this section of the report is used to describe the main difficulties that will be the focus of the psychotherapy (e.g., "the client struggles with depressed feelings and anxiety that interfere with her ability to leave the house", "The client appears to be experiencing a prolonged mourning and grief reaction following the death of her husband 2 years ago", etc.). In this section you may also make note of any diagnoses (past or current) as reported directly by the client; take care to stipulate that this was stated by the client himself or herself (e.g., "It should be noted that the client reported that one of his psychiatrists told him he had borderline personality disorder").

Preliminary Clinical Formulation:

In this section, the clinician describes his or her formulation or clinical understanding of the client, the clinical picture, and/or the symptoms and behaviors that will be the focus of the treatment. The style of your Preliminary Clinical Formulation will be influenced by your theoretical orientation and/or the orientation that you see may best address the situation with the particular client. Thus, a psychodynamic or analytic clinician may place emphasis on the potential underlying conflicts, fantasies and past experiences that may be part of the clinical picture whereas a cognitive-behavioral therapist may place more emphasis on current life events, the development of a particular cognitive style or schema, and learned patterns of responding and behaving. Regardless of one's theoretical orientation, this section should present your views in a somewhat tentative manner – one that acknowledges the preliminary nature of the formulation. Thus again, phrases such as "It appears...", "It seems likely that...", "Though speculative at this time, it seems that the client...", "It may be hypothesized that the client…", are helpful to convey the preliminary nature of this aspect of the report.

Recommendations and Preliminary Treatment Plan:

In this section, the clinician first supplies his or her clinical recommendations. For example, this will include the recommendation that the client be seen in psychotherapy at a certain frequency and for a certain period of time. It may also include the recommendation that the client be referred for such things as psychological testing and/or a psychiatric consultation and/or consultations with other professionals (e.g., a couple or family therapist) or organizations (e.g., social services, employment centers, shelters, etc.). In addition to your recommendation(s), you should also offer some explanation as to why such a recommendation is being made and/or for what particular problem or aspect of the problem (e.g., "A short-term psychodynamic therapy at a frequency of twice per week was recommended so as to help the client better understand and resolve the prolonged mourning over the loss of her husband", "It is recommended that the client commence a cognitive-behavioral treatment at a frequency of once per week to help him address how his cognitive style impacts his panic attacks and phobic avoidance of women"). Here we might also briefly mention the factors that support our recommendation (e.g., "Though the client stated that she found her previous group therapy helpful, she indicated that she is now interested in better understanding how her past experiences with loss are affecting her coping with her current relationship anxieties; thus a psychodynamic approach appears indicated.") In this section you might also sometimes include what is not recommended and why (e.g., "It appears that an individual psychotherapy may, at present, be too emotionally overwhelming for the client given her reported recent erotomanic episode with her previous individual therapist, thus it is recommended that the client receive supportive group therapy".)

Once you have stated your recommendations, it is time to describe the preliminary Treatment Plan. If you have made recommendations for consults with other professionals or organizations, you would here mention how you have facilitated or are going to facilitate this. With respect to any recommendation for treatment that you will be doing with the client, it is here where you mention the goals for treatment and the methods and/or techniques to be used (e.g., "exploration and interpretation of underlying conflicts and fantasies", "bibliotherapy", "relaxation techniques", "mindfulness exercises", "homework assignments", "understanding and exploration of the therapeutic relationship", etc.)

Description of Treatment Contract and Informed Consent / Additional Comments:

The last section of the Intake Report provides documentation regarding the manner in which you explained the treatment recommendations, the nature of the treatment (including what to expect from the treatment), as well as what is expected of the client as part of the treatment contract (e.g., nature of attendance, cancellation policy, fees, etc.). Depending on your particular professional college, order, or licensing body you may be required to have the client read and sign a consent form for treatment; if so, it is here that you explain that you took this measure (as well as keeping a copy of the consent form in the file itself). If a consent form is not used, it is particularly important that you here document that you obtained verbal informed consent from your client.

As with all things documented in your client's file, be sure to include your official signature line and signature.

Patricia C. Baldwin

Patricia C. Baldwin, Ph.D.
Clinical Psychologist

SAMPLE INTAKE REPORT #1

Name: Peter Jones   **Date of Intake Session(s):** April 12, 18, 1997
Date of Birth: May 15, 1953   **Date of Report**: April 19, 1997
Marital Status: Married 7 y.   **Living Arrangement**: lives with spouse & son
Occupation: Teacher   **Home Address**: 222 Shamrock Street,
                                                          Ottawa, Ontario, S12 JFW
Tel. Number(s): 555-555-2121   **OK to leave message?** Yes
Emergency Contact and Number: Jane Smith Jones (wife) 555-777-5544
Referral Source: Dr. Granger (GP)

Brief Description of the Client:

The client appeared on time for both assessment appointments but reported that
he had been very rushed getting to my office. He was polite and appropriate in
his interactions with me. At first he did come across as somewhat anxious and
uncomfortable speaking candidly and shared with me his nervousness about
doing so. By the second assessment session he appeared somewhat more
relaxed and was able to engage more readily. A good preliminary rapport was
established.

Presenting Difficulties:

The client reports feeling very anxious and irritable much of the time and
would like to gain a better understanding of this and "other things" that he has
been dealing with throughout his life. It seemed apparent that the client had
much more he wanted to say about these "other things" but that he was not yet
comfortable doing so. In particular, he expressed a wish to understand and deal
with his issues so as to better address marital problems he has been having.
Specifically, he reports feeling a tremendous amount of, what he referred to
as "irrational and crazy jealousy". He explained that his wife has encouraged
him to seek help for many years and that she has threatened to leave the
marriage on different occasions if he does not change. Though a significant
part of his motivation for seeking treatment at this time appears to be related
to his marital difficulties, he also expressed a wish to understand himself and
what prevents him from being happy and content in his life in general. In

particular, he told me that he is worried that his irritability may affect not only his relationship with his wife and family but also his relationships at work and with friends. He explained that he feels he has been holding in a lot of anger, and that he is afraid he will explode one day if he doesn't take care of it.

History of the Presenting Difficulties:

The client explained that though he has always felt like an anxious person, his anxiety has increased profoundly since marrying his wife 7 years ago. He recalled that everything was going well between them until the first month after their marriage. It was then that he began to experience extreme jealousy regarding other men that his wife paid attention to (in particular, her colleagues at work) and convinced himself that she was going to have an affair and leave him. As he spoke, he communicated an understanding that his suspicions and worries are unfounded, but that despite his attempts at reassuring himself he explained that he remains "paranoid" about his wife's behavior. He had hoped that having children would ease his worries, but found that his anxieties, irritability, and jealousy became somewhat worse when his son was born (5 years ago). He described feeling increasingly left out and distant from his wife after the birth as she was preoccupied with the baby and seemed less interested in him.

Significant Life History and Background Information:

The client is an only child born to immigrant parents from Eastern Europe. He was brought up in a middle class environment and explained that his parents worked very hard so that he could attend the best private schools in the city. His father worked in construction for several years and then returned to school and became a teacher; the client explained that he wanted to "follow in his footsteps" and so pursued a career in teaching as well. During the interview, he described his father in very positive terms as humble, strong, and intelligent, though somewhat remote and distant from his feelings. He explained that although he had a good relationship with him, he had always hoped they could have been closer.

In contrast to his feelings about his father, he reported having a very difficult relationship with his mother who he d escribed as intrusive, suspicious, critical of others and being a "huge worry wart". He felt that she was overprotective and is worried that this has had an impact on him and how he feels about himself and life in general. He further explained that both his parents grew up during the war and that he knows they each went through some very negative experiences but that these remain secrets in the family.

Towards the end of the second assessment session, the client explained that his own parents' marriage had had some difficulties. He explained that they would often fight and that his mother would throw things at his father. The client wasn't certain, but expressed that he thought he once overheard his mother accusing his father of having an affair. He recalled that this worried him terribly and that he himself became convinced that his father was actually in love with a colleague (one of the client's own teachers in elementary school). To this day, the client remains uncertain about his father's fidelity to his mother.

Towards the end of the second session, the client explained that his father is currently undergoing some medical and neurological tests to determine if recent changes in his behaviour (e.g., forgetfulness, outbursts of anger, withdrawal) are related to the beginning of dementia. He is very worried about his father and what this will mean for himself and his mother.

The client described himself as having been a rather unhappy child, something he attributes to having spent much of his time studying at home and not engaging enough with other children. He recalled his sadness hearing other children playing outside in the street while he was being made to go to bed while it was still light out in the summer time. He explained that he felt left out most of the time and derived most of his pleasure through gaining the approval and praise of his teachers in school. Despite his unhappy childhood, the client explained that he eventually became engaged in art work (drawing and cartooning) and that this gave him some joy and a chance to engage with other children who admired his talents. The client remarked that, in general, he has difficulty remembering his childhood experiences.

The client explained that during his adolescence (14-15 years) he recalls having gone through a period of depression and withdrawal that he has never understood. He remembered wanting to stay in his bed all day and not having the energy to go to school. He was too ashamed to tell anyone how sad he had felt. He explained believing that if his mother had known she would have "freaked out and become hysterical", so he tried to keep his feelings to himself. He is not sure how he overcame this period, but remembered feeling very relieved when it was over.

He described his college years as a very positive time in his life and that this corresponds with leaving home and making some very dear friendships. He found leaving his parents' house liberating. He reported experimenting with drugs and alcohol for the first time during college. One very bad experience while taking a strong drug (he did not know what it was) scared him and he swore off doing drugs ever again. As based on his experience (that included some visual hallucinations and distortions in his sense of time, color perception and sense of self) he wonders whether the drug may have been LSD.

The client met his wife 9 years ago having been introduced by a mutual friend. He explained that at first he was not really attracted to her physically but connected with her on an intellectual level. He recalled being drawn to her kindness and the way in which she attended to him. She works as a nurse and he jokingly commented that perhaps he wanted someone to take care of him. He explained that he felt very secure with her up until after they married. In describing their sexual life, though hesitant to speak about this at first, he eventually explained that he struggles with intrusive fantasies about his wife being in bed with other men and that he finds this strangely arousing and upsetting at the same time.

With respect to his work life, the client describes taking great satisfaction in his job. He explained that he has won a number of teaching awards and that he seems to be highly regarded among his colleagues. He tends to feel very pressured to excel and explained that he does not allow himself to make mistakes. He often feels riddled with guilt when he knows he has not done his best and will ruminate about this after a class, sometimes interfering with his ability to work. At times, he explained, he also worries that his colleagues secretly dislike him and that they may do things to "trip him up" or make him look bad in the eyes of their superiors. This leads him to withdraw from others and not share too much about himself at work.

He has not seen a therapist in the past, but has consulted with a medical practitioner for anti-depressant medication that he used during a period of depression and lethargy a few years ago. He and his wife also attended some couple counselling sessions during periods of crisis in the marriage. He reported that he did not find the couple's therapy very useful as he felt the therapist was taking the side of his wife.

Significant Medical History:

The client explained that his physical health is "ok". He suggested that there may be some issues in this area but that he did not feel comfortable discussing them as of yet. I did not pursue this further.

Clinical Observations and Impressions:

The client is a high functioning professional man who experiences anxiety, irritability, and mild obsessional traits (e.g., strong internal demands for efficiency, perfection, intellectualization, self-criticism, guilt) that appear to limit his enjoyment of work and family life. The client also experiences intense feelings of jealousy and is very insecure regarding his wife's fidelity. He does have insight into the exaggerated nature of his suspiciousness and reports that his jealousy is unfounded in fact. There was some suggestion that the client struggles with a more general difficulty trusting others (for example, in the work place). This was also evident during the assessment process itself in that the client was apprehensive about disclosing certain details regarding his life to the therapist. The client appears to be struggling with chronic difficulties with mood and his affective life, having experienced sadness and anxiety throughout much of his childhood and adolescence. Potential underlying core conflicts appear related to issues of trust, anxieties surrounding success, and inhibitions and anxiety surrounding underlying aggressive feelings. The client appears to have a strong need for self-sufficiency and may be uncomfortable depending on others (including the therapist) for assistance. (Note that the client demonstrated some anxiety about self-disclosure during our interviews, and indicated that there are issues that he would prefer to keep private until he feels more comfortable). The client's estimated global assessment of functioning indicates a mild level of difficulty with some problems in relationships, work, or school functioning. The client is nonetheless functioning well and has some significant relationships.

Diagnostic Impressions:

The client's clinical presentation suggests a dysthymic condition with chronic anxiety. Perfectionistic tendencies and some obsessional qualities also appear evident. The client also struggles with suspiciousness regarding others that appear to be interfering with his marital and work relations (he does not, however, meet the criteria for paranoid personality disorder). The client demonstrates insight regarding the exaggerated nature of his suspiciousness of others. A good observing capacity was evident and the client was readily able to engage in a preliminary exploration of the nature of his difficulties. He expressed curiosity about the impact of his childhood experiences in response to some trial interpretations drawing potential links between his past and present struggles. There was no evidence of serious psychopathology or substance abuse difficulties.

Preliminary Clinical Formulation:

The client appears to be struggling with intense jealousy, anxiety, and underlying anger that is possibly related to an identification with his mother's distress that he experienced throughout his childhood (which included her own jealousy and suspicions regarding his father's fidelity). Indeed, he expressed feeing linked to his mother in a "special way" and that he was somehow responsible to take care of her. His experience of his father's emotional detachment and distance from him has also likely contributed to his feelings of worry about the potential loss of love from a much-needed figure. That his father is presently in ill health may be stimulating further his sense of insecurity. The experience of being an only child who often felt left out while others were "having fun" also seems to have contributed to his anxiety about having a secure place with others and possibly with his wife. That his jealousy and worry regarding his wife's fidelity increased after the birth of their child may in some ways relate to a revival of his own childhood jealousies and anxieties with his own parents (worries stimulated by the presence of a relational triangle; mother-father-baby).

There is some suggestion that the client experiences anxiety regarding his underlying aggressive wishes and feelings that he fears will be destructive and come into conflict with his intense wish for approval and acceptance. The client is aware that he has likely been repressing his anger and that this may be contributing to his irritability and feeling that he could "explode". His perfectionism and need to be pleasing to others also appears to come into conflict with his needs for assertion and expression of anger.

The client's suspiciousness regarding others (his wife as well as his colleagues) is another important feature of his character that appears to reflect a more general sense of insecurity regarding basic trust in relationships. This may impact how the client will experience the therapeutic relationship and setting and will be an important avenue for further exploration.

Recommendations and Preliminary Treatment Plan:

Exploratory psychodynamic psychotherapy at a frequency of twice per week with an emphasis on better understanding and working through his anxieties, jealousies, depressive affect, areas of conflict, and coping with his current marital situation is recommended. Increased awareness of the potential links between his marital distress and his experience of his parents' marriage and his own potential identification with his mother will be an important preliminary goal with the aim of helping him resolve his jealousy with respect to his wife. Exploration and working through of painful childhood and adolescent experiences (alluded to during intake) and their links to his current anxiety is also recommended to further his self-understanding and self-acceptance. An exploration of his experience relating to the therapist may provide an important avenue for working through of his more general anxieties regarding trust in relationships.

It is also recommended that the client and his wife pursue couple therapy as an adjunct to the client's individual treatment to deal with their recent and past marital difficulties. Note that I offered a referral source for such services (Harmony Couples and Family Clinic).

Description of Treatment Contract and Informed Consent / Additional Comments:

After an explanation of the nature of a psychodynamic treatment, its goals and methods, alternative treatment approaches and the therapy contract the client consented to beginning a course of twice per week psychodynamic therapy (with the possibility of increased frequency as needed), to be conducted in an open-ended fashion. (Signed consent to treatment is here included). Given that the client will be attending twice weekly sessions, it was agreed that the fee will be reduced to $100.00 per session.

Patricia C. Baldwin

Patricia C. Baldwin, Ph.D.
Clinical Psychologist

SAMPLE INTAKE REPORT #2

Name: Ms. Maxwella Smart   **Date of Intake:** Sept. 15, 2016
Date of Birth: October 22, 1980   **Marital Status:** Single
Living Arrangement: with younger sister **Occupation:** Hair Stylist
Home Address: 55555 Park Street   **Telephone Number:** 555-5556
Apartment 555, Coldwater, Ont.V1S 159
OK to leave message?: yes; private cell
Emergency Contact and Number: 555-252-5555 (Janet Smart; Sister)
Referral Source: Dr. David (Psychiatrist)

Brief Description of the patient:

The patient arrived early to the interview and apologized for ringing the doorbell a number of times. She initially came across as rather overwhelmed and nervous as she struggled to find words to describe her situation. With the therapist's encouragement she was able to explain her difficulties and eventually seemed more at ease.

Presenting Difficulties:

The patient reported that she has been struggling with fears of leaving her home and interacting with others on account of her anxieties about coming into contact with germs and illness. She explained that her difficulties became so intense over the past year that she had to leave her job. She reports that she feels she has to wash her hands several times a day (as much as 50 times in a day). In addition to her fears of contamination and illness, the patient also reported increased sadness and depression since taking her leave from work. She stated that she is seeking therapy to help address her "germ phobia" and depression in conjunction with her psychiatric treatment at a local clinic.

History of the Presenting Difficulties:

The patient explained that though she had always been somewhat fearful of germs and catching diseases, her fears intensified greatly after the sudden death of her young daughter in a car accident 4 years ago. A short time after this traumatic loss, her marital relationships became very strained and she divorced her husband of 5 years. Following these losses, she decided to move in with her younger sister so as to have emotional support and to ease her financial situation.

Significant Life History and Background Information:

The patient was born and raised in Ireland and moved to Canada when she was 12 years of age. She has one younger sister 3 years her junior with whom she has a positive relationship. Her parents moved back to Ireland when the patient was 19 years of age. She described the transition to Canada as very difficult as she felt she had no say in the matter. She described similar feelings about her parents' decision to move back to Ireland (she and her sister insisted on staying in Canada to continue their studies). She reports that she currently has an overall positive relationship with both of her parents, though explained that at times they can be quite controlling (e.g., calling her daily over skype, instructing her about how to live her life).

She met her husband when she was 20 years old and they married shortly after. She explained that he was her "soul mate" and that they were excited to start a family together. Having their daughter was a great joy to the couple and she described their life as being ideal and "perfect". She explained that she felt as though her life ended when their daughter was killed tragically in a car accident. The daughter had been traveling on her way to school on a school bus that was struck by an oncoming car. Her daughter was the only child to die in the accident. The patient was very tearful as she described the incident but was able to contain her emotions as she continued with the interview.

After the death of her daughter she and her husband received grief counseling that she found very helpful. She continued to be treated by the counselor in individual therapy (through her divorce) until the counselor announced that she was being relocated to another city. Though she felt that the counseling helped her with her mourning, she explained that her anxieties about contamination and hand-washing were never addressed.

Significant Medical History:

The patient reported a history of migraine headaches for which she takes some very strong pain medication. She has had these headaches since adolescence.

She is currently taking SSRI medication (Venlafaxine) for depression and anxiety as prescribed and followed by her psychiatrist (Dr. Strangelove). She has been on this medication "on and off" following the death of her daughter. She reports that it has been very helpful and that she experiences few side effects.

Clinical Observations and Impressions:

The patient appears quite distressed and preoccupied by the intrusion of her obsessive-compulsive symptoms. At present, the patient's difficulties are making it difficult for her to work, be with others, and to enjoy her usual activities. Her current symptoms appear to be a continuation of an emotional reaction to the trauma of losing her young child in a tragic accident and the subsequent dissolution of her marriage in the wake of their loss.

Diagnostic Impressions:

The patient is struggling with obsessive-compulsive symptoms involving obsessive thoughts and fears of contamination with the accompanying compulsion to wash her hands repeatedly during the day so as to reduce the anxiety. She also experiences some agoraphobic tendencies that appear secondary to her fear of contamination. These symptoms are accompanied by depressed mood, which, though being treated pharmaceutically, remains significantly disruptive to the patient's functioning. The patient's estimated overall level of functioning suggests some serious emotional and psychological difficulties and quite serious impairment in relational and work functioning (the patient feels unable to work, is currently on an extended work leave, and is struggling to maintain personal relationships due to her anxieties).

Preliminary Clinical Formulation:

The patient's clinical picture appears consistent with an underlying mourning reaction to the several losses she has experienced over recent years. A common theme through the patient's presentation concerns the lack of control, unpredictability and uncertainty that has surrounded so many of her recent (and past) life events. It is possible that her obsessive-compulsive symptoms are a means of exerting an impact, having some power and a sense of control over something in her life (e.g., germs and disease). Her agoraphobic reaction may also be an attempt to exert some control over her life and to keep her "safe" from the outside world, which has come to be experienced as very dangerous. Embarrassment regarding her symptoms also appears to be a factor that is keeping her isolated and withdrawn from others.

Recommendations and Preliminary Treatment Plan:

It is recommended that the patient begin a course of Cognitive-Behavioral treatment to help address her obsessive-compulsive symptoms, depressive affect, and agoraphobic reaction. The treatment plan includes the use of exposure (imaginal and in vivo) and response prevention so as to have the patient habituate to the triggers of her anxiety and to then gradually resist her excessive hand-washing behavior and avoidance of social interaction. Other techniques to be implemented involve self-monitoring of thoughts and feelings surrounding her fears, anxieties, and depressive affect. Throughout the treatment, unresolved feelings regarding the mourning of her daughter's death will also be addressed and explored as needed.

Description of Treatment Contract and Informed Consent / Additional Comments:

After an explanation of the nature of a cognitive-behavioral treatment approach, its goals and methods, alternative treatment approaches and the therapy contract, the client consented to beginning a course of once per week therapy (to be conducted over a 6 month period). The patient supplied her verbal consent to the treatment contract and the 24-hour cancelation policy, and agreed to pay the fee of $150 per session.

Patricia C. Baldwin

Patricia C. Baldwin, Ph.D.
Clinical Psychologist

INTAKE REPORT TEMPLATE

Name: **Date of Intake Session(s):**
Date of Birth: **Date of Report:**
Marital Status: **Living Arrangement**
Occupation: **Home Address:**
Tel. Number(s):   **OK to leave message?:**
Emergency Contact and Number:
Referral Source:

Brief Description of the Client:

Presenting Difficulties:

History of the Presenting Difficulties:

Significant Life History and Background Information:

Significant Medical History:

Clinical Observations and Impressions:

Diagnostic Impressions:

Preliminary Clinical Formulation:

Recommendations and Preliminary Treatment Plan:

Description of Treatment Contract and Informed Consent / Additional Comments:

_____

Signature

Chapter 2

Maintaining a File: The Session Note or Progress Note

Once psychotherapy has begun, a mental health practitioner must keep notes on what transpires during each session. There are specific topics and types of information that such a Progress Note should contain as well as many things it should not. In this chapter, I will first indicate the types of identifying information that begin each Progress Note and then briefly outline the structure of a basic Progress Note that can be used to guide and organize its content. Along the way I will offer some general direction regarding what to include and what not to include in such a note (as derived from the Guidelines of the American Psychological Association and the Canadian Psychological Association; Appendix A also includes a helpful checklist of content to include and content to avoid in your psychotherapy records). This chapter also includes a brief description of the SOAP note format and how to use this method to structure your progress notes. Some sample progress notes and SOAP notes appear at the end of the chapter and in Appendix B, along with some blank templates for your use. A free, downloadable Progress Note template is also available on our website at http://www.notedesigner. com/book/.

Progress Note

Name:	**Fee:**
Date:	**Start time:**
Payment Status:	**Stop time:**

The beginning of your progress note should always include the client's name and date of the session. Though not always strictly required, it is also recommended to include the fee, duration of the session, and a note about the status of the payment (which is of course helpful for your accounting). Some professional bodies in the United States also stipulate that the daily record should include the "start time" and "stop time" of a session as well as the CPT (Current Procedural Terminology) code for service. It should be noted that some professional orders also require that each page of a patient's record include the recording of the patient's name (be sure to check with your own professional body to see if this is the case in your jurisdiction).

Though written headings are not always necessary in your daily progress notes, I do recommend using the "mental headings" outlined below as a guide to help structure and organize the information. The general headings I find helpful and recommend are: Overall Functioning, Affective State, Mental Status, Themes, Interventions, Developments, Treatment Plan, and Ongoing Issues. Each of these sections and what they can include are described below. Another popular method for organizing a note is the Subjective-Objective-Assessment-Plan (SOAP) structure – at the end of the chapter I'll include some guidelines for constructing a SOAP note.

THE BASIC PROGRESS NOTE

Overall Level of Functioning:

It is helpful to begin a note with a short description of the client's overall level of functioning. Here you may include a few statements regarding the level of severity of the client's struggles (I tend to use the approach of the Global Assessment of Functioning Scale from the earlier additions of the DSM as a general guide). For example, "The client's estimated global assessment of functioning suggests a moderate degree of emotional distress and difficulty dealing with relationships, work and/or school life" or "The client's estimated global assessment of functioning suggests that the client is in some danger of harm to self or others and is having serious difficulty maintaining self-care and basic life functioning". For a list of possible statements you can use to describe a client's overall level of functioning see Appendix C.

Affective and Emotional State:

Next, I suggest providing a brief description of the main emotional state(s) evidenced by the client. You might also note whether and in what way his or her emotional state changed over the course of the session. Keep in mind that both negative and positive emotions should be included where appropriate (we tend to focus more on the presence of negative emotions as clinicians). For a list of possible statements you can use to describe a client's affective and emotional state please see Appendix C.

Mental State:

You might also make brief mention of the client's overall mental or cognitive state: For example, whether he or she was able to adopt a reflective stance; whether the client comes across as dissociated from his or her experience; any evidence of confusion, poor judgment, suicidal ideation, hypomanic features, obsessional preoccupation, improved judgment, or perhaps a strong capacity for reflection and insight. For a list of possible statements you can use to describe a client's affective and emotional state please see Appendix C.

Main themes of the session:

Next I suggest listing the main topics and issues that emerged or were discussed and explored by the client. In the interest of keeping a concise note that does not also expose too much of the client's personal information, I suggest using general categories to describe what was explored. For instance, instead of saying that "the client described how on Saturday night she threw a dish on the floor while she and her husband were fighting and that she thought she never should have married him and called him a jerk….etc." you might simply state "The client explored a recent relational conflict with her husband and her difficulties containing her rage and aggressive feelings". By restricting the content to a general overview you are less likely to reveal something in the client's file that may be potentially detrimental to the client's wellbeing if read by a third party (such as when a file is requested by an insurance company or if required by the courts) or by the client himself or herself in the future. For a list of possible statements you can use to describe the main themes of a session, as organized by different categories, please see Appendix C.

There are times when it is important to document in detail what has transpired during a session. This is the case when a client discloses content related to a wish to cause serious harm to self or others, or in the case of possible abuse of a child or other vulnerable person. In such situations, you should carefully document what the client has reported in detail as well as all interventions you took to assess and address the potential crisis. Keep in mind that in the event of any question regarding your management of a case, your documentation is what can protect you in the event of litigation. You must be able to demonstrate that you took all appropriate and reasonable clinical measures to assess the level of risk and protect the client and/or people at risk in a manner consistent with the current standards of the profession.

Main therapeutic interventions:

In order to be accountable for the work we do with clients, it is very important that we document the interventions we make during a session. Thus, in addition to describing the themes and issues raised during the session, we must also make some mention of what we ourselves did during the session to address the client's difficulties. For instance, in the case of a psychodynamic treatment the clinician should mention the types of interpretations made; in cognitive-behavioral therapy, the clinician should mention any techniques suggested and/or homework assignments reviewed or assigned; while in a supportive treatment the clinician should mention any guidance and problem solving help provided to the client. Of course, sometimes our main intervention may simply include active listening and providing some reflective statements regarding the client's experience. Regardless of how active or inactive you have been during a session, it is important to provide some documentation regarding how you intervened and/or whether you chose not to intervene as may be required by the clinical situation. For a list of possible statements you can use to describe the main therapeutic interventions (including supportive, cognitive-behavioral and psychodynamic perspectives) please see Appendix C.

Developments, treatment plan, outlook and ongoing issues:

The last section of your note should make some mention of any significant developments or progress that the client has made as observed in the session or reported by the client (e.g., "The client continues to make steady gains in self-esteem and confidence"). As well, you should here include a brief statement regarding the treatment plan (in particular any changes to the original treatment plan as set out in the Intake Report should be noted). In the case of ongoing psychotherapeutic work where there is no change to the treatment plan we might simply state something like, "The ongoing treatment plan includes continued support and maintenance of the psychotherapeutic process". Finally, it is important to make mention of any outstanding clinical issues (e.g., "The client's help-rejecting behaviors remain a significant therapeutic concern"). For a list of possible statements you can use to describe the main developments, treatment plan, and ongoing therapeutic issues please see Appendix C.

Additional comments:

At the tail end of the note, you may sometimes wish to include further details that you think should be noted from a session: For instance, issues regarding late payment, changes in the therapeutic contract, requests for information, instructions regarding an holiday schedule, or significant up-coming events in the client's life that may have an impact on his or her wellbeing and/or the therapy process.

As with all things documented in your client's file, be sure to include your official signature line and signature.

Patricia C. Baldwin

Patricia C. Baldwin, Ph.D.
Clinical Psychologist

THE SOAP NOTE FORMAT

Another useful technique to use when organizing a progress note is the SOAP note format (Weed, 1964). Here the clinician organizes the note according to the following categories: (S) Subjective, (O) Objective, (A) Assessment, and (P) Plan. The first two categories pertain to all relevant information (subjective and objective) that you've collected about the client during the session. The Assessment section outlines all of your thinking and conceptualization about what has emerged in the session and as based upon the information you've collected (subjective and objective). The last section, Plan, is where the clinician describes the interventions used and any direction given to the client as well as the ongoing treatment plan and any prognostic considerations. What follows is a very brief overview of how to write a therapy note using the SOAP note format: For a truly comprehensive discussion of SOAP notes, I refer the reader to an excellent article by Cameron and turtle-song (2002).

Subjective

Here the clinician begins the note with a few statements regarding the state and experience of the client according to *the client's own perspective*. This includes all relevant information you collect from the client in a session about how he or she is functioning, what he or she is experiencing, how the client describes and sees his or her situation as well as his or her experience of the therapeutic work – all *as described by the client*. We may include such things as our clients' self-described mental and emotional state, experiences with others, and ways of perceiving themselves, their relationships and current difficulties. At times it may be important to use quotations from the client, but only if it really helps clarify and capture what they are experiencing (e.g., the client explained that he is in an existential crisis – "I am Sisyphus endlessly pushing a pile of garbage up a mountain of dirt").

Objective

This section of the note includes the relevant information that you collect from and observe about your client as based on your own professional perspective. This section would include such things as your observations of the client's mental and emotional state, and/or your observations regarding their behaviors and appearance. It is very important that in this section you substantiate your statements with reference to what you have "objectively" observed. For example, "The client appeared severely depressed as evidenced by his reported lack of motivation for work and loss of appetite, slow and laboured speech and tearfulness throughout the session." or "The client's behaviour was suggestive of a reaction to the ongoing abuse of her stimulant medication – she appeared physically agitated, could not sit still, was wringing her hands, and paced around the room throughout the session. She had disclosed that she crushed up her pills and "snorted" them before the session".

Assessment

The assessment section includes your clinical perspective and synthesis as derived from what you observed during the session (using the Subjective and Objective data reported above). Here you would include content such as your evaluation of the client's overall level of functioning, your diagnostic opinions and impressions, formulations regarding any significant developments and any outstanding therapeutic issues and concerns. It is in this section that you can state your clinically informed impressions and ideas while making sure they link with, or at least are compatible with, what you described in the Subjective and Objective sections.

Plan

In this final section of the note, the clinician describes and explains any and all interventions made including any suggestions, psycho-education, or direction given to the client. Here you also include the ongoing treatment plan and goals (e.g., "The ongoing treatment plan includes continued support and maintenance of the psychotherapeutic process") as well as any important revisions to previously documented treatment plans. This is also the section within which to document the progress of the treatment process (e.g., "The client continues to make steady gains in self-esteem and confidence") and the direction it may need to take.

SAMPLE PROGRESS NOTES

Name: Ms. J. Bond   **Fee:** $75

Date: January 30, 2010   **Start Time:** 9:00 am

       Stop Time: 9:50 am

Session Note:

Ms B. came 5 minutes late to her appointment explaining that she was anxious to leave the house today. We first addressed some of her fears about leaving the house and how she was able to eventually feel more relaxed through the use of deep breathing exercises.

The client's estimated global assessment of functioning suggests some serious emotional and psychological difficulties and quite serious impairment in relational, work and/or school functioning. The client's affective and emotional state appeared quite depressed and agitated. The client's mental state included a slowing of thought and reduced mental energy. The main themes of the session were: conflict with family members; exploring relational concerns and issues in the workplace; and difficulties with boundaries and self-assertion. The main therapeutic interventions consisted of: an emphasis on here-and-now functioning; a focus on improved problem solving and coping; an emphasis on developing new homework assignments in collaboration with the client; an emphasis on techniques for the development of greater confidence and self-efficacy; and informing the client of how to reach me by telephone between sessions as needed. The client continues to sustain gains made in reduced self-destructive behavior. The recent crisis appears better contained. The ongoing treatment plan includes: addressing problematic coping strategies and mechanisms; building greater social and interpersonal skills; and adjunctive psychiatric/medical assistance. Treatment continues to show good evolution and development. Treatment to continue as indicated.

Jason Bourne

Jason Bourne., MA.

Psychotherapist

Name: Mr. Peter Jones   **Fee:** $30
Date: June 16, 1952   **Duration:** 50 minutes

Progress Note:

The patient's estimated global assessment of functioning appeared reasonably good with only short lived and expectable reactions to everyday stressful events. The patient shows only slight difficulty in relational and/or work/school functioning. The patient's affective and emotional state appeared calm and reflective. The patient's mental state included good insight and observing capacity. The main themes of the session were: interpersonal difficulties with spouse/partner; exploration of transgenerational traumas; and exploration of conflicts regarding masculinity and issues of male sexuality. The main therapeutic interventions consisted of: exploration of fantasy life in light of ongoing anxieties; exploration of fears of abandonment and loss as experienced in the transference; and exploration and interpretations of inhibitions regarding pleasure and enjoyment. The patient continues to make good progress with self-understanding and self-insight. Developments continue in the areas of family and relational functioning. The patient demonstrates a capacity for greater enjoyment of leisure time and creative projects. The ongoing treatment plan includes continued support and maintenance of the psychotherapeutic process. Treatment to continue as indicated.

Note that the client described an important dream about the therapy that we linked to his anxieties about trusting that the therapist will remember him after termination of the treatment (something we discussed in our last session). The client expressed that he found this exploration very helpful and comforting.

Annie Freud, PsyD.
Licenced Therapist

Name: Jane Doe **Fee:** $50
Date: September 5, 2013 **Duration:** 50 minutes
CPT Code: 90834

Progress Note:

Affective and Mental State: The patient's estimated global assessment of functioning suggests a moderate degree of emotional distress and difficulty dealing with relationships, work and/or school life. The patient's affective and emotional state appeared dysphoric.

Themes of the Session: The main themes of the session were: struggles with social anxiety; working towards improved self-esteem and confidence; and exploration of bodily anxieties and distorted body image.

Therapeutic Intervention: The main therapeutic interventions consisted of: setting goals for the treatment and the session; an emphasis on addressing problematic core beliefs; and the use of role play to help address interpersonal difficulties.

Developments, Treatment Plan, Ongoing Issues: Developments continue in the areas of occupational functioning and achievement. Significant gains in self-assertion and positive self-promotion are evident. The ongoing treatment plan includes therapeutic work on building and maintaining self-esteem and self-confidence. There are no current outstanding therapeutic issues or concerns. Treatment to continue as indicated.

Janet Skinner, MD.
Psychiatrist

THE SOAP NOTE FORMAT

Name: Ms. Doubtfire   **CPT Code:** 90834
Date: 08/09/2015   **Start time:** 1:00 pm
Fee: $120   **Stop time:** 1:50 pm
DSM-V Code: 301.83

Progress Note:

Subjective: The patient described feeling overwhelmed by her work and that she is "losing what are left of [her] marbles". The main themes of the session were: conflict with family members; exploration of parenting concerns; and exploring relational concerns and issues in the workplace. A recent argument with her son was a main concern for the client today – she explained that she feels very misunderstood by him and is fearful that he will come to hate her.

Objective: The client's affective and emotional state appeared panicky and agitated. Her legs were shaking throughout the session and she smoked extensively from her electronic cigarette. At times, her anxiety appeared very intense and she could not remain seated – having to get up from her chair and use the washroom on a number of occasions.

Assessment: The client's estimated global assessment of functioning suggests some serious emotional and psychological difficulties and quite serious impairment in relational, work and/or school functioning. Her responses to the Beck Depression Inventory suggest her depression remains in the moderate range. The client shows reductions in self-destructive behavior. The recent crisis appears better contained.

Plan: The main therapeutic interventions consisted of: a focus on helping the client expand problem solving capacities; an emphasis on helping the client develop greater trust in the therapeutic setting, therapist, and interpersonal relationships; and an emphasis on developing new homework assignments in collaboration with the client. The ongoing treatment plan includes addressing problematic coping strategies and mechanisms; and crisis management and supportive assistance.

Roberta Hartley
Roberta Hartley, Ph.D.
Clinical Psychologist
Dunhill Hospital

PROGRESS NOTE TEMPLATES

Name: **Fee:**
Date: **Duration:**
Payment Status: **Location:**

Overall Level of Functioning:

Affective and Mental State:

Main Themes of the Session:

Main Therapeutic Interventions:

Developments:

Treatment Plan:

Ongoing Issues:

_____

Signature

PROGRESS NOTE TEMPLATES

Name: **Fee:**
Date: **Duration:**
Payment Status: **Start time:**
                                             Stop time:

Subjective (state and experience of client):

Objective (clinical observations):

Assessment (clinical impressions, formulations, therapeutic issues):

Plan (interventions used, treatment plan, clinical developments):

_____

Signature

Chapter 3

Closing a File:

The Termination Summary or Termination Report

At the conclusion of a psychotherapy treatment, mental health professionals should provide an overview of the treatment received and the nature of termination of the therapy. Such a Treatment Summary or Termination Report is essential to write regardless of the length of the treatment and/or the nature of the termination. In what follows is a description of the structure of a Treatment Summary with a brief description of what might be included in such a report. A sample Termination Summary loosely based on a client I had seen several years ago is included at the end of the chapter, along with a blank template for a Termination Summary. A free, downloadable Termination Summary template is also available on our website at http://www.notedesigner.com/book/ .

Summary of the Presenting Difficulties:

To begin the treatment or termination summary, you should start by briefly restating the issues and difficulties that brought the client to treatment. You might here simply restate what you included in the corresponding section of your original Intake Report.

Other Areas Addressed During Treatment:

Next, it is important to include a short description of any other issues, problems or difficulties that emerged during the course of treatment. For instance, "Though the client's presenting difficulties involved a depressive reaction to a recent job loss, during the course of treatment it became evident that the client was also struggling with a number of characterological difficulties that interfered with her ability to establish and maintain friendships with others. These difficulties were also addressed through the course of the treatment".

Overview of the Treatment Process:

It is in this section where the clinician describes the main features, characteristics and development of the treatment process. In the case of long-term treatment durations, it may be helpful to organize this section into "initial phase of the treatment", "middle phase of the treatment" and "termination phase or late phase". Another helpful way of organizing this section may involve structuring the content around the different problem areas addressed (e.g., treatment of the client's binge eating, the treatment and evolution of the client's interpersonal difficulties, the treatment and evolution of the client's post-traumatic stress disorder, the client's work-related coping, etc.) or around the different aspects of the treatment process (e.g., the nature and development of the therapeutic alliance, the evolution of the relationship with the therapist, significant dream work, the exploration and resolution of core conflicts, etc.).

It is important to keep the focus on the development of the treatment itself (those interventions and processes that were part of the treatment) and not solely on the development of the client. That is, you want to here document how and in what way your work with the client was initiated, was maintained, and progressed over the course of the psychotherapy.

As I have emphasized elsewhere, it is also important here to distinguish between what you observed directly from the client versus your own professional hypotheses, conjectures, or inferences. It can be helpful to begin statements with phrases such as "It appeared that...", "It is likely that...", "There was some suggestion that...", "This suggests that...", "It seems possible that...", "The client appeared to experience this as ...."

Nature of the Termination:

In this section you first describe why and how the termination came about (e.g., "It was mutually decided by client and therapist that the goals of the treatment were sufficiently met and that therapy is no longer indicated" or "As the client did not appear to be further benefiting from the treatment, the possibility of terminating the treatment was raised with the client who agreed to setting an end date" or "The treatment was terminated abruptly by the client who called and stated that she no longer wants to attend therapy as she feels uncomfortable discussing her personal problems with a man. After discussing the issue with her on the phone, it was decided that she be referred to a woman therapist"). Next, you may then go on to describe the termination process itself. For instance, this may include the client's reactions to ending the treatment (e.g, anger, sadness, fear, excitement, a feeling of accomplishment, etc.), any further issues that were stimulated by the ending of the relationship with the therapist (e.g., revisiting feelings of mourning and loss, fears of independence and loneliness, etc.), any problematic features of the termination (e.g. "The client explained that she was too distressed to attend the last session and cancelled at the last minute"), as well as positive features of the termination (e.g., "The client expressed deep appreciation for the therapy process", "The client experienced the termination as a symbolic graduation and beginning of a new journey in his life", etc.).

Gains and Progress Made:

In this section, the clinician outlines all of the gains and progress made by the client throughout the course of treatment. It is important to include both what the client perceived and may have stated as gains and progress as well as what you as a clinician have observed in the client (the two need not always be the same, though there is usually some correspondence between the two). Be sure to include concrete examples of changes and progress made when deemed appropriate and fitting.

Limitations of the Treatment:

It is important to make some statement regarding any limitations of the treatment. No treatment meets all the therapeutic needs of a client and not all clients can benefit from a recommended treatment. It is in this section that the clinician turns an evaluative eye on the treatment conducted and describes the ways in which it was not able to address the treatment goals. Be careful here not slip into a tone that inadvertently blames the client for the limitations of the treatment. Again, the focus is on the treatment itself and not the "limitations" of clients.

Remaining Difficulties and/or Concerns:

In this section, you briefly describe and discuss any remaining difficulties that were either not addressed during the treatment or that were not sufficiently addressed and resolved during the course of treatment. In addition, it is here that you may raise any concerns you have regarding the client's ongoing and future functioning and/or life situation.

Recommendations:

Following from the last section, the clinician here makes any necessary recommendations that may benefit the client. Typically, these are the recommendations that you made to the client in the final phase or final sessions of the treatment. For instance, you may recommend that the client pursue a different form of therapy in the future, or you may suggest that the client will continue to benefit from some form of psychotherapeutic support in the community, or you may simply state that no further recommendations appear indicated. If you have made follow-up recommendations, you should also explain that you have discussed these with the client or relevant person involved (e.g., his or her GP) and the measures you took or are taking to facilitate the recommendation when appropriate. Again, as with all documentation in a client's file, be sure to include your signature line and signature.

Patricia C. Baldwin

Patricia C. Baldwin, Ph.D.
Clinical Psychologist

SAMPLE TERMINATION SUMMARY #1

Name: Mr. Carlo Jonese
Date of Termination Summary: Nov. 3, 2012
Date of First Consultation: Nov 5, 2011
Date of Last Consultation: Nov 2, 2012
Duration of the Treatment: One year

Summary of the Presenting Difficulties:

The client is a 35 year-old man of Italian origin who, at the time of consultation, had recently left home to live with his girlfriend (whom he plans to one day marry). The client sought psychotherapy for feelings of social discomfort and a life-long experience of feeling that he cannot express himself. He had explained that this was interfering with his work life and he feared it would limit his ability to advance in his profession (business consultant). He also described periods of intense anxiety that came on suddenly and which sometimes led to panic attacks. These periods of anxiety began shortly after having decided to move in with his girlfriend of 3 years. He explained that he grew up in a very traditional Italian household and that leaving home before marriage was frowned upon and created conflict between him and his parents as well as with his girlfriend. This was his first consultation with a mental health professional, having no previous experiences in psychotherapy.

Other Areas Addressed During Treatment:

Through the course of treatment, it became evident that the client was experiencing serious insomnia. Addressing his insomnia also became a focus of our work together. Issues of mourning and grief surrounding the death of his girlfriend's father (who died mid-way through our work together) also became an important focus of the treatment.

Overview of the Treatment Process:

The client was seen on a once per week basis in supportive-dynamic psychotherapy with the incorporation of cognitive-behavioral techniques to address his panic attacks and insomnia. A good therapeutic alliance was easily established and maintained throughout the course of our work together. Though the client's presenting difficulty included a subjective sense of not being able to express his thoughts and feelings, our early work revealed that he was, in fact, quite an insightful, emotionally sensitive, and expressive person who, when given sufficient space, could articulate his inner state quite clearly. Continued exploration of this revealed that there had long been a lack of "psychological space" in which he could express himself and listen to his own needs and desires.

During the initial phase of treatment, the client gained significant awareness regarding his psychological/emotional position within his family of origin - as "translator", "mediator" and "go-between" and how this was re-enacted in different triangular relationships in his present life that were causing him distress (e.g., girlfriend-himself-mother; girlfriend-himself-friend; father-himself-uncle). Working through of his sense of responsibility for "keeping the peace" allowed him to disentangle from this pattern and freed him to begin to better tend to his own needs. Improvements in his relational life (with family and friends) were evidenced following this period of therapeutic work.

Another major focus of the treatment was support of the client's movement toward greater emotional autonomy and psychological independence from his family of origin and building of his sense of himself as an adult/man. In exploring this area, it became evident that the client felt strong underlying pressure to fulfill the family's expectation and aspirations for him and that he had set aside his own wishes and desires in response. His moving out of the family home was found to represent an important attempt at asserting his need for independence that conflicted with the emotional demand to fulfill the desires of his family. His panic attacks also appeared to be linked to the intense guilt and conflict he experienced over leaving his family of origin. His panic attacks were however addressed more specifically via psycho-education regarding the panic response, self-monitoring of precipitating thoughts and emotional responses, and the employment of relaxation techniques (i.e., deep breathing and muscle relaxation exercises). Over time, the client was able to better clarify and separate his authentic desires and wishes from those tied to (his experience of) the expectations of those around him. Preliminary working through of this issue helped the client better understand his dissatisfaction in working for the family business and led to an important re-examination of his career goals. It should be noted that the client was extremely over qualified for the type of work he was doing in the family business and his talents and potentials were being underutilized.

Another important aspect of the therapy involved support of the client's coping and self-care during the terminal illness and eventual death of his girlfriend's father, to whom he was also very attached. Therapy provided a place within which he could express and explore his own grief, while being available as support to his bereaved girlfriend. That the death of his girlfriend's father also led him to experience worry and sadness regarding the potential death of his own parents was also explored.

Through the course of treatment it became evident that the client experienced significant insomnia (sleeping only 3 or 4 hours per night and feeling very restless). The onset of his sleep difficulties was found to be linked to a particular work related stress that involved having to fire a number of employees. His anxieties about asserting his authority were explored in this regard. To address his insomnia, the client was provided information on "sleep hygiene" and relaxation techniques that included a combination of guided imagery and progressive muscle relaxation. He also began a workout regime (self-initiated) that he found very satisfying and which had a positive impact on his sleep in a short period of time.

Nature of the Termination:

The client experienced significant improvement and gains throughout the treatment. He expressed the wish to terminate treatment based on feeling satisfied with his level of improvement and the beginning of new life projects that will place new demands on his time and finances (e.g., new career plans, up-coming engagement with girlfriend). A termination date was set for January 30th 2012. The client did not attend his planned termination session, but called to express his appreciation for our work together and to say good-bye.

Gains Made/Progress:

The client made significant gains during the course of treatment and reported being satisfied with his progress. Early on, he came to appreciate and value his capacity to express his needs, thoughts, and feelings once feeling entitled to do so. He also experienced enhanced relational functioning with family and friends following a period of working through of underlying feelings of responsibility for other's feelings and his role as "mediator" between those in conflict. Throughout the course of therapy, the client gained greater awareness of a tendency to neglect his own needs and wishes and developed improved balance between his work, relationship life, and leisure/creative/play time. The client was also able to use the space of the therapy to explore and better clarify his career aspirations and the factors that had been preventing him from making decisions in this regard. The supportive features of the therapy appeared to be very helpful in enhancing the client's coping with his girlfriend's depression and their loss of her father. The behavioral and cognitive interventions appeared to adequately address the client's difficulties with panic and insomnia, both of which were fully resolved by the end of treatment. Overall, the client's mood and self-confidence appeared to improve over the course of treatment. The client reported feeling a new-found sense of freedom and was satisfied with our work together. The client's estimated "global assessment of functioning" at the end of treatment appeared to be in the "high functioning" range with minimal symptoms upon termination.

Limitations of the treatment:

Though explored to some extent during our sessions, the therapy did not sufficiently address the client's underlying conflicts regarding his cultural identity (e.g., his wish to better establish his own positive Italian identity).

Remaining difficulties and/or concerns:

There were no significant remaining difficulties or concerns observed or expressed by the client at the end of treatment.

Recommendations:

Though the client made tremendous progress and met his main goals during the course of treatment, in the interest of maximizing his psychological wellbeing and self-understanding, the client may benefit from ongoing exploratory psychodynamic/analytic therapy in the future.

Follow-up:

No specific follow-up plan is indicated; the client was informed he is free to contact me in the future if needed.

Additional Comments:

Note that the client has one outstanding bill (for the month of January) and has arranged to send this payment by the end of February.

Patricia C. Baldwin

Patricia C. Baldwin., Ph.D.
Clinical Psychologist

SAMPLE TERMINATION SUMMARY #2

Name: Ms. Maxwella Smart
Date of Termination Summary: March 20, 2017
Date of First Consultation: September 15, 2016
Date of Last Consultation: March 16, 2017
Duration of the Treatment: Six months

Summary of the Presenting Difficulties:

The patient presented with obsessive-compulsive symptoms involving extreme anxiety regarding contamination by germs and contracting illnesses and disease from others. Her symptoms led her to avoid social situations and made it impossible for her to continue with her work as a hair stylist. She had also experienced a significant depression that was being treated with anti-depressant medication at the time of consultation. Her symptoms occurred in the context of the traumatic death of her young daughter in an automobile accident and the dissolution of her marriage shortly after their loss.

Other Areas Addressed During Treatment:

Through the course of the treatment it came to light that the patient required further support and assistance with her mourning process. Though our sessions offered important support for the patient's sadness and grief concerning the loss of her daughter, she was also referred to a support group for parents grieving the loss of a child.

Overview of the Treatment Process:

The initial period of treatment focused on establishing rapport and providing emotional support for the patient's immediate concerns. Following this, the treatment focused more directly on implementing Cognitive-Behavioral techniques to help address her Obsessive-Compulsive symptoms. More specifically, the patient was guided in the use of imaginal exposure to the triggers of her anxiety (i.e., germs, dirt, touching surfaces, touching people, being with others). This was accompanied by the use of deep breathing exercises and visualization to help reduce anxiety. As the patient was able to better master her anxiety regarding such imagined triggers, the treatment then introduced in vivo exposure to her triggers (e.g., engaging socially, hand shaking, shopping). Along with the exposure phase of the treatment, the patient was also helped to gradually develop better tolerance for her anxiety reactions and to develop cognitive techniques (self-talk, visualization) so as to help her modify her response to her anxiety. Through the use of these techniques, the patient was able to significantly reduce her compulsive hand washing to a comfortable frequency of 10 times per day.

In addition to the above focus, the patient also engaged in a journal–writing procedure in which she recorded the situations that led her to feel anxious, her interpretations and her reactions and worked on how to develop new ways of responding. Through this procedure the patient was helped to better understand how her interpretations of events (as dangerous, and life threatening) were fueling her fears and that alternative interpretations are also possible. Through this exercise, fears of death related to the trauma of her daughter's accident became better clarified and the patient worked with the therapist to further address her mourning and the impact it has had on her way of experiencing the world and her own life.

Nature of the Termination:

The treatment was terminated after six months by mutual agreement due to the success of the interventions and the patient's confidence in being able to manage on her own.

Gains and Progress Made:

Over the course of treatment the patient was able to significantly reduce her excessive hand-washing behavior (from over 50 times per day to 10 times per day and in response to normal situations) and to reduce her anxieties regarding contamination by germs and contracting diseases and illnesses from others. During the fourth month of treatment the patient was gradually able to resume her work activities and had begun to engage in greater social interaction. A significant improvement in her depressive symptoms was also experienced and the patient is beginning to taper down the dosage of her anti-depressant medication under the supervision of her psychiatrist.

Limitations of the Treatment:

Though the patient experienced a significant reduction in her obsessive-compulsive symptoms, depression, and avoidance of social interaction, she continues to struggle with a complex mourning reaction in the wake of the traumatic death of her young daughter. The patient was able to speak more openly and freely about her sadness and the fears aroused by the death of her daughter through the course of treatment. The treatment did not, however explicitly focus on her mourning process.

Remaining Difficulties and/or Concerns:

Unresolved mourning over the traumatic loss of her daughter, the ending of her marriage, and the many changes these events, in turn, also evoked, remains an important area in need of additional help and support. This was discussed with the patient who was encouraged to continue to pursue her support group for grieving parents and to also seek ongoing individual psychotherapy.

Recommendations:

It is recommended that the patient continue to seek the support of her group for grieving parents and to also pursue a supportive-psychodynamic psychotherapy to help her better work through the traumatic loss of her daughter. Ongoing psychiatric treatment and support from her psychiatrist at the clinic is also recommended.

Patricia C. Baldwin

Patricia C. Baldwin, Ph.D.
Clinical Psychologist

TERMINATION SUMMARY TEMPLATE

Name: **Date of Termination Summary:**
Date of First Consultation: **Date of Last Consultation:**
Duration of the Treatment:

Summary of the Presenting Difficulties:

Other Areas Addressed During Treatment:

Overview of the Treatment Process:

Nature of the Termination:

Gains Made/Progress:

Limitations of the treatment:

Remaining difficulties and/or concerns:

Recommendations:

Follow-up:

Additional Comments:

_____

Signature

Afterword

I hope that these guidelines have helped you in initiating and effectively managing the documentation of your psychotherapy treatments. Though writing appropriate treatment notes can seem daunting and anxiety provoking at first, once you establish a rhythm and habit of quickly and efficiently maintaining your files, it will no longer have to take up more time than is warranted. For those of you who may be similar to my colleague who, for some time, eschewed clinical note writing altogether, I especially hope that you are now more encouraged to begin pursuing this essential task without undue anxiety and hardship. As mental health professionals we have an ethical responsibility to document our work, conduct and interventions with our clients. Without such accountability we are at risk of jeopardizing our professionalism and the trust and confidence of the public that we serve. In addition to this professional duty, I believe there is also great benefit to our own work when we can review and examine our techniques and interventions, treatment successes and treatment failures, with different clients and allow this to inform how we approach new clinical situations and challenges. I wish you all the best with your clinical note writing and your never-ending development and growth as a mental health professional.

Resources and References

Here are some further resources that you may find helpful in the pursuit of professional record keeping.

American Psychological Association. (2007). Record keeping guidelines. *The American Psychologist*, 62(9), 993.

Bemister, T. B., & Dobson, K. S. (2011). An updated account of the ethical and legal considerations of record keeping. *Canadian Psychology/Psychologie canadienne*, 52(4), 296-309.

Cameron, S., & turtle-song, i. (2002). Learning to write notes using the SOAP format. *Journal of Consulting and Development, 80*, 286-292.

Canadian Psychological Association (2001). *Practice Guidelines For Providers of Psychological Services.* The Canadian Psychological Association.

Levin, C., Furlong, A., & O'Neil, M. K. (Eds.) (2003). *Confidentiality: Ethical perspectives and clinical dilemmas.* NJ: Analytic Press.

Ordre des Psychologues du Quebec (2001). Le Dossier du Client. *Psychologie Quebec (Fiche deontologique),* 2 (4), 1-4.

Weed, L.L. (1964). Medical records, patient care, and medical education. *Irish Journal of Medical Education,* 6, 271-282.

Appendix A

**A summary of what to include and what to avoid
in your Psychotherapy Progress Notes and Records**

INCLUDE

- Client's identifying information
- Emergency contact person
- Fees for service
- Dates of service
- Referral source
- Informed consent for treatment
- Informed consent for any disclosures
- Presenting difficulties
- Medications used
- Clinical impressions (diagnoses if mandated)
- Goals of the treatment
- All recommendations and referrals made (including the reasons for them)
- Type of treatment, techniques, and interventions implemented
- Progress and gains made or lack thereof
- Treatment plan and ongoing treatment plans
- All risk behaviors and issues of safety (danger to self and/or others)
- All clinical measures taken in the event of crises (e.g., risk to self and/or others)
- Assessment of safety concerns and how you handled them (all interventions made)
- Observations regarding child abuse, abuse of a dependent, or elder abuse (and any actions you took or did not take and why)
- Consultations with other professionals
- Duration of services rendered
- Treatment compliance
- Nature of the Termination and its impact and management

AVOID

- Personal opinions and feelings
- Derogatory comments
- Countertransference feelings
- Opinions outside of your expertise
- Conjecture stated as fact
- Non-clinically relevant details
- Unsubstantiated judgments
- Names of individuals (unless relevant to crisis management)

Appendix B

Example Progress Notes
(Using Note Designer Software)

Name: Ms. J. Bird   **Fee:** $75
Date: January 30, 2010   **Duration:** 50 minutes

Session Note:

The patient's estimated global assessment of functioning suggests some serious emotional and psychological difficulties and quite serious impairment in relational, work and/or school functioning. The patient's affective and emotional state appeared quite depressed and agitated. The patient's mental state included a slowing of thought and reduced mental energy.

The main themes of the session were: conflict with family members; exploring relational concerns and issues in the workplace; ongoing work toward greater self-empathy; and ongoing work towards greater mindfulness.

The main therapeutic interventions consisted of: an emphasis on here-and-now functioning; a focus on improved problem solving and coping; an emphasis on developing new homework assignments in collaboration with the patient; discussion and establishment of plans and goals for better self-care; and informing the patient of how to reach me by telephone between sessions as needed.

The patient shows reductions in self-destructive behavior. The recent crisis appears better contained. The ongoing treatment plan includes: addressing problematic coping strategies and mechanisms; building greater social and interpersonal skills; and adjunctive psychiatric/medical assistance. Treatment continues to show good evolution and development. Treatment to continue as indicated.

Anna Oh., Ph.D.
Clinical Psychologist

Name: Jane Doe   **Fee:** $50
Date: September 5, 2013   **Duration:** 45 minutes

Progress Note:

The patient's affective and emotional state appeared sad and withdrawn. The patient's mental state included improved reflective capacity. The main themes of the session were coping with feelings of rejection in interpersonal relationships, and awareness and exploration of underlying needs for care and support. The main therapeutic interventions consisted of setting goals for the treatment and the session, and the use of role play to help address interpersonal difficulties. Significant gains in self-assertion and positive self-promotion are evident. The ongoing treatment plan includes therapeutic work on building and maintaining self-esteem and self-confidence; and building greater social and interpersonal skills. There are no current outstanding therapeutic issues or concerns. Treatment to continue as indicated.

Maxwell Smart, Ph.D.
Clinical Psychologist

Name: Mr. Sullen
Date: August 8, 2015
Session Duration: 60 minutes
Session Fee: $100

Session Note:

Mr. Sullen came to the session 15 minutes late and explained that he had just received an upsetting text message from his girlfriend who had canceled their dinner date. The main themes of the session were: coping with feelings of rejection in interpersonal relationships; exploration of emotional neglect experienced during childhood/adolescence; and awareness and exploration of deficits in self-preservation. The main therapeutic interventions consisted of: cognitive-behavioral techniques; an emphasis on addressing problematic core beliefs; and addressing the patient's tendency toward all-or-nothing thinking and how this impacts perceptions. There is continued development of the patient's capacity for self-care and life management. The patient demonstrates greater capacity for thought and reflection. The ongoing treatment plan includes building greater social and interpersonal skills; and adjunctive psychiatric/medical assistance. Treatment to continue as indicated.

Mary Poppins
Mary Poppins, Ph.D.
Clinical Psychologist

Name: Mr. Bee
Date: 08/09/2015
Session Fee: $120
Duration: 50 minutes

Progress Note:

Affective and Mental State: The client's estimated global assessment of functioning indicates a mild level of difficulty with some problems in relationships, work, or school functioning. The client is nonetheless functioning well and has some significant relationships.

Themes of the Session: The main themes of the session were: sexual difficulties and/or concerns; exploration of mid-life identity concerns and meaning; and exploration and working through of inner self-criticism, self-punishment and self-denial.

Therapeutic Intervention: The main therapeutic interventions consisted of: a review of therapeutic work done in previous sessions; the use of imagery to address fears and anxieties; and an emphasis on the implementation and practice of relaxation techniques.

Developments, Treatment Plan, Ongoing Issues: The client demonstrates a growing capacity for greater pleasure in relationships and work. The ongoing treatment plan includes therapeutic work on building and maintaining self-esteem and self-confidence; and addressing problematic coping strategies and mechanisms. There are no current outstanding therapeutic issues or concerns. Treatment to continue as indicated.

Barney Fife, Ph.D.
Clinical Psychologist
Montreal Therapy Centre

Name: Ms. Dora
Date: August 9, 2015
Session Fee: $90

Progress Note:

Subjective: The main themes of the session were: working through interpersonal/ family experiences; interpersonal difficulties with spouse/partner; sexual difficulties and/or concerns; and exploration of impact of sexual abuse experiences experienced in childhood/adolescence.

Objective: The patient's affective and emotional state appeared rather distressed, nervous and irritable.

Assessment: The patient's estimated global assessment of functioning suggests a moderate degree of emotional distress and difficulty dealing with relationships, work and/or school life. A significant reduction in symptoms continues. The patient continues in process of re-working and alleviation of traumatic pain and stress.

Plan: The main therapeutic interventions consisted of: an emphasis on strengthening self-care and self-preservation; an emphasis on evaluation and exploration of problematic automatic thoughts; the use of imagery to address fears and anxieties; helping overcome overgeneralization in patient's cognitive style; and focus on social skills enhancement and practice. The ongoing treatment plan includes: therapeutic work on building and maintaining self-care; better understanding the impact of the patient's traumatic history on present day relationships and experiences; and support of the patient's adaptive defenses and/or coping capacities.

Peter Rabbit, Ph.D.
Psychologist/Psychoanalyst

Appendix C

Progress Note Sample Statements
(Excerpted from Note Designer Software)

OVERALL LEVEL OF FUNCTIONING

The client's estimated global assessment of functioning...

- appeared to be superior in most areas of life with no indication of emotional difficulty or distress. The client is not overwhelmed by life's difficulties and is able to enjoy relationships, work/school, and leisure time.
- appeared to be very good with minimal difficulties and is able to cope well in most areas of life (e.g., relationships, work/school, and leisure). The client is quite content and reports only everyday difficulties and concerns.
- appeared reasonably good with only short lived and expectable reactions to everyday stressful events. The client shows only slight difficulty in relational and/or work/school functioning.
- indicates a mild level of difficulty with some problems in relationships, work, or school functioning. The client is nonetheless functioning well and has some significant relationships.
- suggests a moderate degree of emotional distress and difficulty dealing with relationships, work and/or school life.
- suggests some serious emotional and psychological difficulties and quite serious impairment in relational, work and/or school functioning.
- indicates the client is struggling with very serious emotional and psychological difficulties that appear to be interfering with perceptions, judgment, thinking, communication and mood. The client is showing severe difficulties in most areas of life (e.g., relationships, work and school life).
- suggests that the client's behavior may be influenced by severe psychological difficulties, delusions and/or hallucinations and is unable to function in most areas of life (e.g., self-care, relationships, work life).
- suggests that the client is in some danger of harm to self or others and is having serious difficulty maintaining self-care and basic life functioning.

- suggests that there is a persistent and serious risk of causing harm to self or others.

AFFECTIVE STATE

The client's affective and emotional state appeared...

- generally positive
- generally content
- calm and reflective
- improved
- mainly unhappy
- sad
- dysphoric
- rather distressed
- mildly depressed
- moderately depressed
- quite depressed
- marked by hopelessness
- withdrawn
- detached
- somewhat flat
- rather flat
- nervous
- mildly anxious
- moderately anxious
- quite anxious
- panicky
- agitated
- over-stimulated
- excited
- irritable
- angry
- enraged
- regressed
- uncontained
- labile
- tired

MENTAL STATE

The client's mental state included…

- good insight and observing capacity
- strong reflective functioning
- improved reflective capacity
- some capacity for reflection
- poor capacity for reflection
- good judgment
- improved judgment
- impaired judgment
- concrete thinking with little capacity for abstraction
- a slowing of thought and reduced mental energy
- inhibition of thought and associations
- obsessional preoccupation
- dissociative features
- phobic preoccupation
- a post-traumatic reaction
- a potential underlying psychotic process
- some deficits in reality testing
- serious reality testing deficits
- confusion and disorganization of thought
- hypomanic features
- manic features
- suicidal ideation/fantasy

THEMES

The main themes of the session were…

Relational:

- relational difficulties
- recent relational conflict
- coping with relational frustrations
- struggles with social anxiety

- coping with anger and envy in interpersonal relationships
- coping with feelings of rejection in interpersonal relationships
- difficulties with boundaries in interpersonal relationships
- securing appropriate boundaries
- crisis situation in family
- conflict with family members
- working through interpersonal/family experiences
- interpersonal difficulties with spouse/partner
- sexual difficulties and/or concerns
- exploration of family life
- exploration of relationship with father
- exploration of relationship with mother
- exploration of relationships with sibling(s)
- exploration of relationships with children
- exploration of parenting concerns
- exploration of relationships with friends
- exploring relational concerns and issues in the workplace
- coping with conflict with authorities at work
- exploring relational concerns and issues in school
- exploration of positive interpersonal experiences
- recent positive relational experiences

Trauma:

- expression of stressful experiences
- exploration and discussion of recent traumatic experiences
- exploration of childhood traumas and neglect
- exploration of multiple traumatic events and cumulative trauma in childhood/adolescence
- exploration of impact of sexual abuse experiences experienced in childhood/adolescence
- exploration of emotional neglect experienced during childhood/adolescence
- exploration of transgenerational traumas
- exploration of vicarious traumatic experiences
- exploration of health concerns and illness
- exploration of end of life anxieties, fears, and concerns

Identity:

- exploration of low self-esteem and poor confidence
- working towards improved self-esteem and confidence
- exploration of bodily anxieties and distorted body image
- conflicts and concerns regarding ethnic/cultural identity
- exploration of anxieties regarding sexual identity and gender
- exploration of conflicts regarding masculinity and issues of male sexuality
- exploration of conflicts regarding femininity and issues of female sexuality
- exploration of conflicts and anxieties regarding masculinity
- exploration of conflicts and anxieties regarding femininity
- exploration of obstacles to identity development in adolescence
- exploration of adolescent identity concerns
- expression and exploration of crisis of identity
- working towards integration of adult identity
- exploration of mid-life identity concerns and meaning
- exploration of late-life identity formation and concerns
- life-review as part of later-life identity consolidation
- expression and exploration of discontinuities in self-state experiences
- difficulties with boundaries and self-assertion
- awareness and exploration of deficits in self-preservation
- exploration of feelings of lack of entitlement
- working towards securing a 'right to a life,' appropriate entitlement and independence
- exploration and working through of 'false-self' states and their relationship to early life experiences
- exploration of guilt feelings and inhibitions regarding pleasure and success

Process:

- exploration of life experiences and self-understanding
- expression and development of 'true self' experiences and enhanced authenticity
- development of self-care and self-preservation
- development of inner security
- ongoing work toward greater self-empathy
- ongoing work towards greater mindfulness
- exploration and working through of inner self-criticism, self-punishment and self-denial

- working through and exploration of inhibitions regarding success and accomplishment
- exploration of conflicts regarding entitlement and self-validation
- exploration of dream life
- exploration of fantasy life
- exploration of the therapeutic relationship
- ongoing working through of transferences
- exploration of characterological and interpersonal difficulties as revisited within the therapeutic relationship
- continued exploration of the impact of early life on current identity
- expression and discussion of problematic beliefs and schemas
- exploration and evaluation of target behaviors and areas of concern
- discussion of medication and its impact
- exploration and discussion of recent homework assignments
- review of the therapeutic work to date
- exploration of therapeutic goals and aims
- revision of therapeutic goals and aims

Mourning/Loss:

- expression and exploration of recent loss
- continued working through of traumatic losses
- continued mourning of childhood losses
- exploration of unhappy childhood experiences and losses throughout life

Adjustment:

- transition to adulthood and adult responsibilities
- strain of mid-life transitions
- coping with recent changes in family life
- late-life adjustment and coping with age-related changes
- adjustment to recent motherhood
- adjustment to recent fatherhood
- parenting anxieties and concerns
- adjustment to separation from child/children
- work life and occupational concerns
- coping with stress at school
- adjustment to university life and studies
- adjustment to new demands in life situation

- adaptation to physical illness
- coping with physical pain and related difficulties

Daily Life:

- management and coping with daily life
- structuring of daily life and making plans for the future
- coping with day to day organizational difficulties
- dealing with self-care (e.g., eating, sleeping, finances)
- dealing with inhibitions regarding help seeking and turning to others for support
- working towards the further development of hobbies and constructive leisure activities
- working toward improved health life style
- how to create better balance between work, relational, recreational, and self needs
- development of greater self-assertion and effective interpersonal communication

Specific Difficulties:

- dealing with panic and anxiety states
- exploration and coping with depression and sadness
- awareness and exploration of feelings of powerlessness, hopelessness and helplessness
- exploration of capacity to return to work
- coping with and management of impulses to self-mutilate
- coping with and management of impulses to self-harm
- coping with suicidal thoughts and feelings
- coping with exhaustion and burn out in work activities
- working through and management of anorectic behavior and related difficulties
- coping and working through of difficulties with chronic binge eating
- exploration and coping with obesity and related eating difficulties
- coping with and working through of drug dependence and abuse
- coping with and working through of addictions and related concerns
- exploration of sleep disturbance
- coping with sexual difficulties
- awareness and exploration of possible psychosomatic reactions

- awareness and exploration of perfectionistic tendencies
- issues of impulse control and containment of affects
- awareness and exploration of underlying aggression and feelings of rage
- exploration and working through of guilt and related anxieties
- exploration of anxieties regarding healthy dependency
- awareness and exploration of underlying needs for care and support
- awareness and exploration of tendency to push others away in response to anxiety
- exploration and working through of difficulties with trust in interpersonal relationships
- development of internal self-care and maternal self-function
- development and working toward greater creativity and capacity for play
- development of expanded spiritual and creative experience
- development of occupational functioning and pleasure in work activities

THERAPEUTIC INTERVENTIONS

The main therapeutic interventions consisted of...

Supportive:

- supportive techniques
- an emphasis on the establishment and maintenance of the therapeutic frame
- an emphasis on self-expression
- an emphasis on here-and-now functioning
- an emphasis on containment of affect
- an emphasis on coping with current life difficulties
- a focus on improved problem solving and coping
- an emphasis on containment of recent regressive episode
- a focus on impulse control and anger management
- a focus on containment of acting-out behavior
- a focus on helping the client expand problem solving capacities
- an emphasis on strengthening self-care and self-preservation
- developing and maintaining the therapeutic alliance so as to facilitate and foster continued therapeutic work
- an emphasis on helping the client develop greater trust in the therapeutic setting, therapist, and interpersonal relationships
- an emphasis on clinical management

Cognitive Behavioral:

- cognitive-behavioral techniques
- an emphasis on evaluation and exploration of problematic automatic thoughts
- setting goals for the treatment and the session
- targeting more effective problem solving and coping skills in daily life
- an emphasis on addressing problematic core beliefs
- evaluating and addressing dysfunctional thoughts
- reviewing and exploring homework assignments
- a review of therapeutic work done in previous sessions
- an evaluation and exploration of target issues and behaviors
- an exploration of feedback regarding previous sessions
- an emphasis on developing new homework assignments in collaboration with the client
- addressing the impact of current medications and their effects
- the use of role play to help address interpersonal difficulties
- the use of imagery to address fears and anxieties
- exploration and planning of in vivo exposure to help address anxieties and fears
- helping overcome overgeneralization in client's cognitive style
- addressing the client's tendency toward all-or-nothing thinking and how this impacts perceptions
- addressing and working to help client overcome the tendency to engage in catastrophization
- exploration of underlying schemas that impact thought and behavior
- an emphasis on the implementation and practice of relaxation techniques
- an emphasis on self-monitoring of thoughts, emotions and behavior
- Socratic questioning or guided discovery to help client address mental style
- providing client feedback regarding development and progress
- an emphasis on techniques for the development of greater confidence and self-efficacy
- an emphasis on self-assertiveness and confidence building
- an emphasis on the development of greater mindfulness and reflective capacity

Psychoanalytic/Psychodynamic:

- psychodynamic techniques
- exploration of fantasy life in light of ongoing anxieties
- exploration and interpretations of the transference
- exploration of fears of abandonment and loss as experienced in the transference
- exploration of fears of rejection and judgment as experienced in the transference
- exploration of the client's underlying sexual wishes and desires
- exploration of the client's underlying aggressive wishes and impulses
- psychodynamic listening
- exploration and interpretation of anxieties regarding boundaries within the therapeutic relationship and the frame
- exploration and interpretation of dream material with emphasis on awareness of underlying anxieties, desires and wishes
- interpretations of dream material with emphasis on manifest content and its relationship to current conflicts and concerns
- exploration and interpretations regarding possible resistances
- exploration and interpretations of underlying sexual anxieties and conflicts
- exploration and interpretation of underlying anxieties regarding loss and abandonment
- exploration and interpretation of underlying anxieties regarding fear of punishment, physical threat, and/or retaliation
- exploration and interpretation of underlying anxieties regarding destructive impulses and wishes
- exploration and interpretation of underlying annihilation anxiety and fears of fragmentation
- exploration and interpretations of underlying fears of engulfment and merger in relationships
- addressing defenses against aggressive impulses and desires
- addressing defenses against sexual impulses and desires
- exploration and interpretations of inhibitions regarding pleasure and enjoyment
- exploration and interpretations of inhibitions regarding self-expression and assertion
- an emphasis on support of defenses to contain impulse life and regressive experiences

- an emphasis on support of defenses to help contain regressive experiences
- exploration and interpretation of possible physical manifestations of psychic conflict and pain
- exploration and interpretation of psychosomatic concerns and difficulties
- exploration of self-destructive motives underlying acting-out behavior
- exploration of suicidal impulses in relation to unacknowledged and unmetabolized anger
- exploration and interpretation of projections that are interfering with social and interpersonal functioning

Other Interventions:

- discussion and establishment of plans and goals for better self-care
- a focus on anger management and containment of acting out
- exploration of appropriate interaction and communication
- focus on social skills enhancement and practice
- discussion of better life management and organization of projects
- exploration of means of overcoming phobic avoidance
- psychoeducation and instruction regarding panic attacks and their management
- instruction and management of sleep difficulties
- supportive psychoeducation regarding recovery from psychosis
- discussion of plans for drug cessation
- continued psychoeducation on addictions and their management
- discussion of ways of managing current crisis situation
- establishing a plan of how to proceed in the event of a suicidal crisis
- informing the client of how to reach me by telephone between sessions as needed

SIGNIFICANT DEVELOPMENTS

- The client continues to make good progress with self-understanding and self-insight
- There is continued development of the client's capacity for self-care and life management
- Developments continue in the areas of family and relational functioning
- Developments continue in the areas of occupational functioning and achievement
- Developments continue in the areas of healthy separation and interdependence

- Developments continue in the area of containment of harmful acting out behavior
- The client continues to make steady gains in self-esteem and confidence
- The client shows reductions in self-destructive behavior
- A significant reduction in symptoms continues
- The client demonstrates a growing capacity for greater pleasure in relationships and work
- The client demonstrates a capacity for greater enjoyment of leisure time and creative projects
- The client shows an enhanced capacity for parenting and improved parenting of children
- Significant gains in self-assertion and positive self-promotion are evident
- The client displays enhanced feelings of appropriate entitlement
- Continued improvement in maintenance and respect of boundaries is evident
- The client continues to sustain gains made in reduced self-destructive behavior
- Developments are being made in the therapeutic alliance
- The client continues in process of re-working and alleviation of traumatic pain and stress
- The client continues to gain greater mastery over traumatic stimuli and fears
- The client demonstrates greater capacity for thought and reflection
- The recent crisis appears better contained
- The client is in a regressive period
- Recent crisis appears to be overwhelming client's current resources
- Planning for termination is underway
- Termination process is in progress

ONGOING TREATMENT PLAN

The ongoing treatment plan includes...

- continued support and maintenance of the psychotherapeutic process
- continued support of the client's self-exploration and understanding
- support of the client's capacity for thought and reflection
- building and development of safety and trust in the relationship with the therapist
- therapeutic work on building and maintaining self-esteem and self-confidence
- therapeutic work on building and maintaining self-care

- therapeutic interventions aimed at helping with target behaviors and difficulties
- addressing problematic coping strategies and mechanisms
- building greater social and interpersonal skills
- adjunctive psychiatric/medical assistance
- continued exploration of meaning and significance of client's difficulties in light of past relational patterns and underlying beliefs
- continued exploration of current life difficulties in light of early childhood experiences
- helping the client gain greater awareness of underlying fantasies, wishes, and fears
- exploration of meaning and significance of the client's difficulties in light of psychic conflict
- better understanding the impact of the client's traumatic history on present day relationships and experiences
- helping the client gain greater awareness, understanding, and expression of underlying emotions
- therapeutic work on understanding, containment and management of self-destructive impulses and/or behaviors
- management of uncontained affects and drive states
- support of the client's adaptive defenses and/or coping capacities
- crisis management and supportive assistance
- movement towards termination of the treatment process
- planning for termination of the treatment

OUTSTANDING THERAPEUTIC ISSUES AND CONCERNS

- There are no current outstanding therapeutic issues or concerns
- Self-destructive wishes and behaviors remain a significant therapeutic concern
- Resistance to treatment recommendations remains a significant concern
- The client's help-rejecting behaviors remain a significant therapeutic concern
- The client's current regressive state is a significant concern
- Treatment continues to show good evolution and development
- Treatment to continue as indicated

CPSIA information can be obtained
at www.ICGtesting.com
Printed in the USA
LVHW040229060123
736553LV00003B/493